The Best *of* Chief Dan George

Publishers Note: This book preserves the original words of Chief Dan George, reflecting the language and terminology of his time. While some terms are no longer considered appropriate today, they remain unchanged to honor his voice, historical context, and the integrity of his message. They also serve as a reminder of where we once were and how far we have come since.

The Best *of* Chief Dan George

by Chief Dan George

Illustrations by Helmut Hirnschall

Copyright © 2004 Chief Dan George & Helmut
2025 Reprint

Cataloguing data available from Library and Archives Canada
9780888395443 [paperback]

9780888392985 [hardback]

9780888391902 [epub]

All rights reserved. No part of this publication may be reproduced, stored in a retrieval system or transmitted, in any form or by any means, electronic, mechanical, audio, photocopying, recording, or otherwise (except for copying permitted by Sections 107 and 108 of the U.S. Copyright Law and except for book reviews for the public press), without the prior written permission of Hancock House Publishers. Permissions and licensing contribute to the book industry by helping to support writers and publishers through the purchase of authorized editions and excerpts. Please visit www.accesscopyright.ca.

Illustrations and photographs are copyrighted by the artist or the Publisher unless stated otherwise.

Printed in Korea

Cover Design: E. Morton
Editor: D. Martens
Design & Layout: E. Morton

We acknowledge the support of the Government of Canada through the Canada Book Fund and the Canada Council for the Arts, and of the Province of British Columbia through the British Columbia Arts Council and the Book Publishing Tax Credit.

 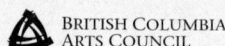 

Supported by the Province of British Columbia

Published simultaneously in Canada and the United States by

HANCOCK HOUSE PUBLISHERS LTD.
19313 Zero Avenue, Surrey, B.C. Canada V3Z 9R9
288 Martin St, Box 10 [Suite 6], Blaine, WA, USA 98230
www.hancockhouse.com | info@hancockhouse.com

Hancock House gratefully acknowledges the Halkomelem Speaking Peoples whose unceded, shared and asserted traditional territories our offices reside upon.

THANKS

To my father:
For he gave me skill, stamina
and the knowledge of my past.

To my mother:
For she gave me the love for life
and taught me to respect it.

To my wife:
Because she shared my burden
when it threatened to slow
my pace and kept by my side when
we travelled lightly.

To my children and their children:
Because in their eyes
I have seen myself.
This is good.

CONTENTS

Biographical Sketch *by Harriett Shlossberg* — 11
The Lament for Confederation *by Chief Dan George* — 15

MY HEART SOARS

My Mother — 18
Young People — 18
Words to a Grandchild — 20
Of All the Teachings We Receive — 28
Touch a Child — 29
The Sunlight — 30
No Longer — 31
If You Talk to Animals — 32
O Earth — 33
I Am a Native of North America — 34
Feelings — 38
Faster — 39
I Have Sat Many Hours — 40
The Young and the Old — 46
Keep a Few Embers — 46
Walk Softly — 47
I Have Known You — 48
For Thousands of Years — 50
The Wisdom and Eloquence of My Father — 51
A Man Who Lives and Dies in the Woods — 52
Look at the Faces of My People — 52
After the Winter's Cold — 54
Signs of New Life — 54
The Beauty of the Trees — 56
My People's Memory — 59
There Is a Longing in the Heart of My People — 61

MY SPIRIT SOARS

Friendship	64
Never Have the Animals	65
Have I Left the Eagle to Soar in Freedom?	66
There Is a Longing	67
Prayer for My Brother the Bear	68
The Bear Is Closest to Man	69
The Empty Loon's Nest	70
My Face Is the Land	73
I've Tried to Be an Indian	76
A Child's Trust	79
Let Nature Be	80
The Only Thing	81
To a Native Teenager	83
When Death Comes	87
The Earth Waits for Me	88
A Man	89
The Wolf	91
The Wolf Ceremony	91

Life	94
Love I	95
The Great Spirit	97
If Your Soul Should Choose a Tree	97
I Never Scorned God	98
The Sun	101
A Bit of Sunshine	101
I Wish	102
Wisdom	104
The Grace of God	105
A Child	106
Let Someone Else	108
To a Child	111
I Would Be a Sad Man	111
Men	112
Love II	113
The Drum Has Fallen Silent	114
Once More	115
Epilogue	116

BIOGRAPHICAL SKETCH

by Harriett Shlossberg

CHIEF DAN GEORGE, accomplished performer, poet, philosopher, champion of First Nations peoples, loving patriarch of a large family, was born in 1899 on a Salish Band reserve on Burrard Inlet, in North Vancouver, one of twelve children of the chief. His given name was Teswahno, meaning "thunder coming up over the land from the water." Like most native children at that time, under the influence of the Catholic Church and in need of white culture's education, he went to a residential school at the age of five, so as not to be separated from his cherished older brother Harry. The next eleven years were difficult ones, being distanced from family, culture, language and customs. Schooling ended at sixteen, and he went immediately into the forest to harvest trees. At nineteen, in an arranged marriage, he and a sixteen-year-old Squamish girl, Amy, entered into a devoted union of fifty-two years' duration. They had eight children, six of whom survived into adulthood. Dan worked as a longshoreman off and on for the next twenty-seven years, during frequent strikes supplementing his income with hunting and lumbering, until he had a serious accident on the docks in 1947, which damaged a hip and leg. In the '40s, with his children and a cousin, who billed themselves as Dan George and His Indian Entertainers, he played for dances three or four nights a week throughout British Columbia. Travelling and sleeping in a covered truck, they would spend the summers picking hops and performing country and western music, with the kids doing special requests for extra money. Dan's instrument was the bass fiddle. He always remembered those years as the happiest times in his life.

Chief Dan George working on a canoe. Photo: Anthony Carter

During the '50s, he was occupied with the duties of chief for his band. In the early 1960s, CBC TV was producing a series called *Caribou Country*. When an actor fell ill, the search was on to find a replacement for a character called Ol' Antoine. Through a fateful series of connections, Chief Dan tested for, and won, the part. With no formal training, he slipped into an instinctive way of acting that won him much acclaim, though initially he had to overcome a measure of hesitation and doubt. Having his two sons in the acting world was a major support, as was Amy's whole-hearted encouragement. Chief Dan gained further national recognition in 1967 with his now famous speech, *The Lament for Confederation*, which he read at the Centennial celebration in Vancouver. That same year, he came to the attention of the playwright George Ryga, who was working on his powerful drama, *The Ecstasy of Rita Joe*. Their meeting resulted in the full development of the character of Rita Joe's father, which Chief Dan played, first at the Playhouse in Vancouver, and then two years later at the National Arts Centre in Ottawa, to glowing reviews. He also appeared in the Royal Winnipeg Ballet production based on the play. In 1973, he would recreate the part in Washington, D.C., for overflow audiences.

When an episode of Paul St. Pierre's *Caribou Country* was bought by a Hollywood studio, Chief Dan got a call to test for the character Ol' Antoine in the Walt Disney movie, *Smith*. He easily got the part, and so began a film career that reached its peak with his legendary performance of the role of Old Lodgeskins, in Arthur Penn's film *Little Big Man*, with Dustin Hoffman, in 1970. For the first time, Indigenous people were seen without the stereotypical bias the film industry had reflected for the first seventy years of its history. Chief Dan received the New York Film Critics' Award and the National Society of Film Critics' Award, as well as an Oscar nomination for the depth and sincerity of that characterization. For the last ten years of his life, he was in demand as a spokesperson for Indigenous people, and as an actor, musician, writer, speechmaker. He even toured for a year with the rock band Fireweed. Many awards came to him, including an honorary Doctor of Laws from Simon Fraser University. His highest aim was always for better understanding by white people of his culture and his people, and he pursued this with determination, wisdom and courage. He died in Vancouver in 1981.

Chief Dan George with Dustin Hoffman in Little Big Man, *1969.*
Photo: The Bettmann Archive

*These words were spoken by Chief Dan George,
a hereditary Chief of the Coast Salish tribe and honorary
Chief of the Squamish tribe of British Columbia.
This speech was given at Canada's Centennial celebration
in Vancouver in 1967.*

THE LAMENT FOR CONFEDERATION
by Chief Dan George

How long have I known you, oh Canada? A hundred years? Yes, a hundred years. And many many "seelanum" more. And today, when you celebrate your hundred years, oh Canada, I am sad for all the Indian people throughout the land.

For I have known you when your forests were mine, when they gave me my meat and my clothing. I have known you in your streams and rivers where your fish flashed and danced in the sun, where the waters said come, come and eat of my abundance. I have known you in the freedom of your winds. And my spirit, like the winds, once roamed your good lands.

But in the long hundred years since the white man came, I have seen my freedom disappear like the salmon going mysteriously out to sea. The white man's strange customs which I could not understand, pressed down upon me until I could no longer breathe.

When I fought to protect my land and my home, I was called a savage. When I neither understood nor welcomed this way of life, I was called lazy. When I tried to rule my people, I was stripped of my authority.

My nation was ignored in your history textbooks—they were little more important in the history of Canada than the buffalo that ranged the plains. I was ridiculed in your plays and motion pictures, when I drank your firewater, I got drunk—very, very drunk. And I forgot.

Oh Canada, how can I celebrate with you this Centenary, this hundred years? Shall I thank you for the reserves that are left to me of my beautiful forests? For the canned fish of my rivers? For the loss of my pride and authority, even among my own people? For the lack of my will to fight back? No! I must forget what's past and gone.

Oh, God in Heaven! Give me back the courage of the olden Chiefs. Let me wrestle with my surroundings. Let me again, as in the days of old, dominate my environment. Let me humbly accept this new culture and through it rise up and go on.

Oh, God! Like the Thunderbird of old I shall rise again out of the sea; I shall grab the instruments of the white man's success—his education, his skills, and with these new tools I shall build my race into the proudest segment of your society. Before I follow the great Chiefs who have gone before us, oh Canada, I shall see these things come to pass.

I shall see our young braves and our chiefs sitting in the houses of law and government, ruling and being ruled by the knowledge and freedom of our great land. So shall we shatter the barriers of our isolation. So shall the next hundred years be the greatest and proudest in the proud history of our tribes and nations.

MY HEART SOARS

MY MOTHER

My mother had a kindness
that embraced all life.
She knew her place well
and was comfortable in giving
everything she had.

This is the tradition
of native women.

YOUNG PEOPLE

Young people
are the pioneers
of new ways.
Since they face
too many temptations
it will not be easy
to know what is best.

WORDS TO A GRANDCHILD

Perhaps there will be a day
you will want to sit by my side
asking for counsel.
I hope I will be there
but you see
I am growing old.
There is no promise
that life will live up to our hopes
especially to the hopes of the aged.
So I write of what I know
and some day our hearts
will meet in these words
—if you let it happen.

In the midst of a land
without silence
you have to make a place for yourself.
Those who have worn out
their shoes many times
know where to step.
It is not their shoes
you can wear
only their footsteps
you may follow
—if you let it happen.

You come from a shy race.
Ours are the silent ways.
We have always done all things
in a gentle manner,
so much as the brook
that avoids the solid rock
in its search for the sea
and meets the deer in passing.
You too must follow the path
of your own race.
It is steady and deep,
reliable and lasting.
It is you
—if you let it happen.

You are a person of little,
but it is better to have little
of what is good,
than to possess much
of what is not good.
This your heart will know
—if you let it happen.

Heed the days
when the rain flows freely,
in their greyness
lies the seed of much thought.
The sky hangs low
and paints new colors
on the earth.

After the rain
the grass will shed its moisture,
the fog will lift from the trees,
a new light will brighten the sky
and play in the drops
that hang on all things.
Your heart will beat out
a new gladness
—if you let it happen.

Each day brings an hour of magic.
Listen to it!
Things will whisper their secrets.
You know what fills the herbs with goodness,
makes days change into nights,
turns the stars
and brings the change of seasons.

When you have come to know
some of nature's wise ways
beware of your complacency
for you cannot be wiser than nature.
You can only be as wise
as any man will ever hope to be
—if you let it happen.

Our ways are good
but only in our world.
If you like the flame
on the white mans' wick,
learn of his ways,
so you can bear his company,
yet when you enter his world,
you will walk like a stranger.
For some time
bewilderment will,
like an ugly spirit,
torment you.
Then rest on the holy earth
and wait for the good spirit.
He will return with new ways
as his gift to you
—if you let it happen.

Use the heritage of silence
to observe others.
If greed has replaced the goodness
in a man's eyes
see yourself in him
so you will learn to understand
and preserve yourself.
Do not despise the weak,
it is compassion
that will make you strong.
Does not the rice
drop into your basket
whilst your breath
carries away the chaff?
There is good in everything
—if you let it happen.

When the storms close in
and the eyes cannot find the horizon
you may lose much.
Stay with your love for life
for it is the very blood
running through your veins.
As you pass through the years
you will find much calmness
in your heart.

It is the gift of age,
and the colors of the fall
will be deep and rich,
—if you let it happen.

As I see beyond the days of now
I see a vision:
I see the faces of my people,
your sons' sons,
your daughters' daughters,
laughter fills the air
that is no longer yellow and heavy,
the machines have died,
quietness and beauty
have returned to the land.
The gentle ways of our race
have again put us
in the days of the old.
It is good to live!
It is good to die!
—This will happen.

OF ALL THE TEACHINGS WE RECEIVE

Of all the teachings we receive
this one is the most important:

Nothing belongs to you
of what there is,

of what you take,
you must share.

TOUCH A CHILD

Touch a child—
they are my people.

THE SUNLIGHT

The sunlight does not leave its marks
on the grass.
So we, too, pass silently.

NO LONGER

No longer
can I give you a handful of berries as a gift,

no longer
are the roots I dig used as medicine,

no longer
can I sing a song to please the salmon,

no longer
does the pipe I smoke make others
sit with me in friendship,

no longer
does anyone want to walk with me to
the blue mountain to pray,

no longer
does the deer trust my footsteps ...

IF YOU TALK TO ANIMALS

If you talk to animals they will talk with you
and you will know each other.

If you do not talk to them you will not know them,
and what you do not know you will fear.

What one fears one destroys.

O EARTH

O earth
for the strength
in my heart
I thank Thee.

                O cloud
                for the blood
                in my body
                I thank Thee.

        O fire
        for the shine
        in my eyes
        I thank Thee.

                O sun
                for the life
                you gave to me
                I thank Thee.

I AM A NATIVE OF NORTH AMERICA

IN THE COURSE OF MY LIFETIME I have lived in two distinct cultures. I was born into a culture that lived in communal houses. My grandfather's house was eighty feet long. It was called a smoke house, and it stood down by the beach along the inlet. All my grandfather's sons and their families lived in this large dwelling. Their sleeping apartments were separated by blankets made of bull rush reeds, but one open fire in the middle served the cooking needs of all. In houses like these, throughout the tribe, people learned to live with one another; learned to serve one another; learned to respect the rights of one another. And children shared the thoughts of the adult world and found themselves surrounded by aunts and uncles and cousins who loved them and did not threaten them.

My father was born in such a house and learned from infancy how to love people and be at home with them.

And beyond this acceptance of one another there was a deep respect for everything in nature that surrounded them. My father loved the earth and all its creatures. The earth was his second mother. The earth and everything it contained was a gift from See-see-am ... and the way to thank this great spirit was to use his gifts with respect.

I remember, as a little boy, fishing with him up Indian River and I can still see him as the sun rose above the mountain top in the early morning ... I can see him standing by the water's edge with his arms raised above his head while he softly moaned ... "Thank you, thank you." It left a deep impression on my young mind.

And I shall never forget his disappointment when once he caught me gaffing for fish just for the fun of it. "My Son," he said. "The Great Spirit gave you those fish to be your brothers, to feed you when you are hungry. You must respect them. You must not kill them just for the fun of it."

This then was the culture I was born into and for some years the only one I really knew or tasted. This is why I find it hard to accept many of the things I see around me.

I see people living in smoke houses hundreds of times bigger than the one I knew. But the people in one apartment do not even know the people in the next and care less about them.

It is also difficult for me to understand the deep hate that exists among people. It is hard to understand a culture that justifies the killing of millions in past wars, and is at this very moment preparing bombs to kill even greater numbers. It is hard for me to understand a culture that spends more on wars and weapons to kill, than it does on education and welfare to help and develop.

It is hard for me to understand a culture that not only hates and fights his brothers but even attacks nature and abuses her. I see my white brothers going about blotting nature from his cities. I see him strip the hills bare, leaving ugly wounds on the face of mountains. I see him tearing things from the bosom of Mother Earth as though she were a monster, who refused to share her treasures with him. I see him throw poison in the waters, indifferent to the life he kills there; and he chokes the air with deadly fumes.

My white brother does many things well for he is more clever than my people, but I wonder if he knows how to love well. I wonder if he has ever really learned to love at all. Perhaps he only loves the things that are his own but never learned to love the things that are outside and beyond him. And this is, of course, not love at all, for man must love all creation or he will love none of it. Man must love fully or he will become the lowest of the animals. It is the power to love that makes him the greatest of them all ... for he alone of all animals is capable of love.

Love is something you and I must have. We must have it because our spirit feeds upon it. We must have it because without it we become weak and faint. Without love our self esteem weakens. Without it our courage fails. Without love we can no longer look out confidently at the world. Instead we turn inwardly and begin to feed upon our own personalities and little by little we destroy ourselves.

You and I need the strength and joy that comes from knowing that we are loved. With it we are creative. With it we march tirelessly. With it, and with it alone, we are able to sacrifice for others.

There have been times when we all wanted so desperately to feel a reassuring hand upon us ... there have been lonely times when we so wanted a strong arm around us ... I cannot tell you how deeply I miss my wife's presence when I return from a trip. Her love was my greatest joy, my strength, my greatest blessing.

I am afraid my culture has little to offer yours. But my culture did prize friendship and companionship. It did not look on privacy as a thing to be clung to, for privacy builds up walls and walls promote distrust. My culture lived in big family communities, and from infancy people learned to live with others.

My culture did not price the hoarding of private possessions; in fact, to hoard was a shameful thing to do among my people. The Indian looked on all things in nature as belonging to him, and he expected to share them with others and to take only what he needed.

Everyone likes to give as well as receive. No one wishes only to receive all the time. We have taken much from your culture ... I wish you had taken something from our culture ... for there were some beautiful and good things in it.

Soon it will be too late to know my culture, for integration is upon us and soon we will have no values but yours. Already many of our young people have forgotten the old ways. And many have been shamed of their Indian ways by scorn and ridicule. My culture is like a wounded deer that has crawled away into the forest to bleed and die alone.

The only thing that can truly help us is genuine love. You must truly love us, be patient with us and share with us. And we must love you—with a genuine love that forgives and forgets ... a love that forgives the terrible sufferings your culture brought ours when it swept over us like a wave crashing along a beach ... with a love that forgets and lifts up its head and sees in your eyes an answering love of trust and acceptance.

This is brotherhood ... anything less is not worthy of the name.

I have spoken.

FEELINGS

They say we do not show our feelings.
This is not so.

Everything is within,
where the heart pounds out the richness
of our emotions.

The face only speaks
the language of the passing years.

FASTER

Faster
the drum sounds
as the spirits move closer

the rattle shakes
and we dance.

I HAVE SAT MANY HOURS

I have sat many hours
on the steps outside my house,
and while I whittled
I tasted nature
and felt her throb of life.
Yet the strangers walking by
thought me lazy.

We all wander through life
united by the bond of creation
and become brothers
through gratitude.
We have much to be thankful for.
Let each of us
talk to the same Supreme Being
in his own way.

A man who cannot give thanks
for the food he eats
walks without the blessings of nature.

Once people knew how to live in harmony;
now the silence of nature
reaches few.

There are many who look,
but only some who see.

The earth is holy,
the feet that walk on it are blessed.

If the legends fall silent,
who will teach the children
of our ways?

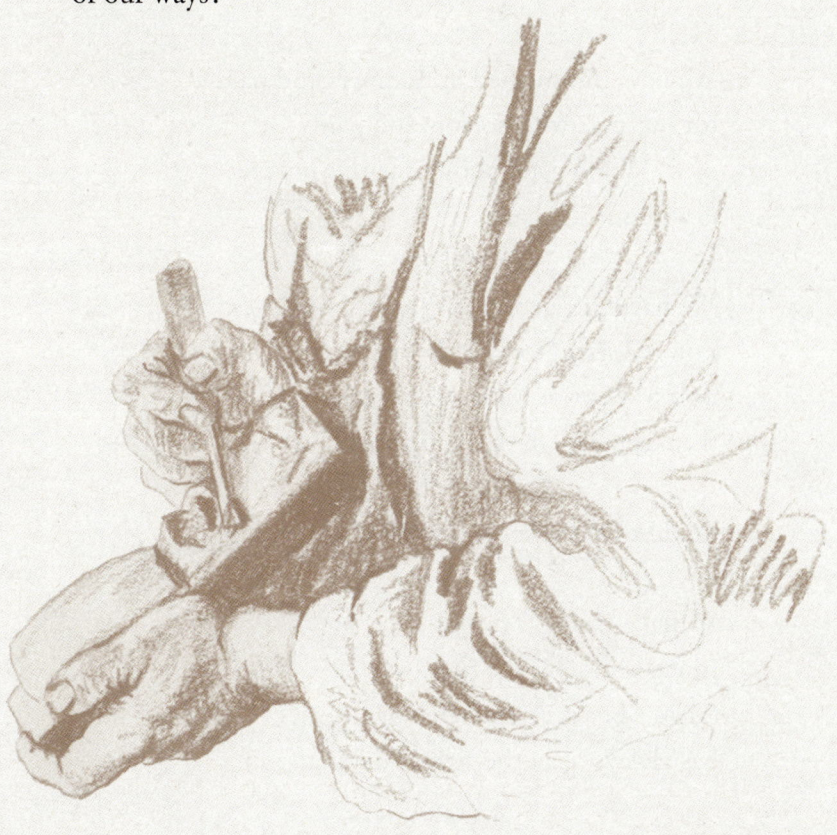

When a man sits down in quietness
to listen to the teachings of his spirit
many things will come to him
in knowledge and understanding.
We have been so much luckier
because we never needed to communicate
in any other way than by thought or word.

This alone will no longer be possible.

We have diminished in numbers and paid
for our past with sorrow and pain
of which no generation of native people
is without its share.

We have suffered much,
now we stand to lose all
unless we preserve whatever is left
from the days of our ancestors.

To do this, the spoken word is not enough.

When a thought forms
it needs much time to grow.
Silence between spoken words
has always been the sign of deliberation.

In these new times of a modern world
where everything has become of value
silence has become time.
Time unused has become time wasted.
We are told: "Time is money."

It is harder to find somebody
who will listen, but everybody reads.
Therefore we must write about our ways,
our beliefs, our customs, our morals,
how we look at things and why,
how we lived, and how we live now.

To do this, we need
the old and the young.

Soon there will be many books
that will tell of our ways
and perhaps will shame even those
who think us inferior
only because we are different.
To those who believe in the power
of the written word these books
will proclaim our cultural worth.
It has been done so for other races
and their teachings.
This is how our young people
will bring to you the true image
of our native people
and destroy the distortion
of which we have been victims
for so long.
Then we will prosper in all things.
From our children will come those braves,
who will carry the torches to the places
where our ancestors rest.
There we will bow our heads
and chant the song of their honor.
This is how the void will be filled
between the old and the new ways.

THE YOUNG AND THE OLD

The young and the old are closest to life.
They love every minute dearly.

If the very old will remember,
the very young will listen.

KEEP A FEW EMBERS

Keep a few embers
from the fire
that used to burn in your village,
some day go back
so all can gather again
and rekindle a new flame,
for a new life in a changed world.

WALK SOFTLY

Walk softly,
follow my footsteps
'til we meet at dawn.

    Stand quietly,
    let your lips give praise
    to the new sun.

I HAVE KNOWN YOU
I have known you
when your forests were mine;
when they gave me my meat
and clothing.
I have known you
in your streams
and rivers
where your fish flashed
and danced in the sun,
where the waters said come,
come and eat of my abundance.
I have known you
in the freedom of your winds.
And my spirit,
like the winds,
once roamed your good lands.

FOR THOUSANDS OF YEARS

For thousands of years
I have spoken the language of the land
and listened to its many voices.
I took what I needed
and found there was plenty for everyone.
The rivers were clear and thick with life,
the air was pure and gave way
to the thrashing of countless wings.
On land, a profusion of creatures abounded.
I walked tall and proud
knowing the resourcefulness of my people,
feeling the blessings of the Supreme Spirit.

I lived in the brotherhood of all beings.
I measured the day
by the sun's journey across the sky.
The passing of the year was told
by the return of the salmon
or the birds pairing off to nest.
Between the first campfire and the last
of each day I searched for food,
made shelter, clothing and weapons,
and always found time for prayer.

THE WISDOM AND ELOQUENCE OF MY FATHER

The wisdom and eloquence of my father
I passed on to my children,
so they too acquired faith,
courage, generosity, understanding,
and knowledge in the proper way of living.
Such are the memories of yesterday!
Today, harmony still lives in nature,
though we have less wilderness,
less variety of creatures.
Fewer people know the cougar's den
in the hills, nor have their eyes followed
the eagle's swoop, as he writes endless
circles into the warm air.
The wild beauty of the coastline
and the taste of the sea fog remains hidden
behind the windows of passing cars.
When the last bear's skin has been taken
and the last ram's head has been mounted
and fitted with glass eyes,
we may find in them the reflection
of today's memories.
Take care, or soon our ears will strain
in vain to hear the creator's song.

A MAN WHO LIVES AND DIES IN THE WOODS

A man who lives and dies in the woods knows the secret life of trees.

LOOK AT THE FACES OF MY PEOPLE

Look at the faces of my people:
You will find expressions of love and despair, hope and joy, sadness and desire, and all the human feelings that live in the hearts of people of all colors. Yet, the heart never knows the color of the skin.

AFTER THE WINTER'S COLD

After the winter's cold and icy winds, life again flows up from the bosom of Mother Earth. And Mother Earth throws off dead stalks and withered limbs for they are useless. In their place new and strong saplings arise.

SIGNS OF NEW LIFE

Already signs of new life are arising among my people after our sad winter has passed. We have discarded our broken arrows and our empty quivers, for we know what served us in the past can never serve us again.

THE BEAUTY OF THE TREES

The beauty of the trees,
the softness of the air,
the fragrance of the grass,
speaks to me.

The summit of the mountain,
the thunder of the sky,
the rhythm of the sea,
speaks to me.

The faintness of the stars,
the freshness of the morning,
the dew drop on the flower,
speaks to me.

The strength of fire,
the taste of salmon,
the trail of the sun,
And the life that never goes away,
They speak to me.

And my heart soars.

MY PEOPLE'S MEMORY

My people's memory
reaches into the
beginning of all things.

THERE IS A LONGING IN THE HEART OF MY PEOPLE

THERE IS A LONGING in the heart of my people to reach out and grasp that which is needed for our survival. There is a longing among the young of my nation to secure for themselves and their people the skills that will provide them with a sense of worth and purpose. They will be our new warriors. Their training will be much longer and more demanding than it was in olden days. The long years of study will demand more determination; separation from home and family will demand endurance. But they will emerge with their hand held forward, not to receive welfare, but to grasp the place in society that is rightly ours.

I am a chief, but my power to make war is gone, and the only weapon left to me is speech. It is only with tongue and speech that I can fight my people's war.

Oh, Great Spirit! Give me back the courage of the olden Chiefs. Let me wrestle with my surroundings. Let me once again, live in harmony with my environment. Let me humbly accept this new culture and through it rise up and go on. Like the thunderbird of old, I shall rise again out of the sea; I shall grab the instruments of the white man's success—his education, his skills. With these new tools I shall build my race into the proudest segment of your society. I shall see our young braves and our chiefs sitting in the houses of law and government, ruling and being ruled by the knowledge and freedoms of our great land.

This talk has been good!

MY SPIRIT SOARS

Friendship lives in every heart.

NEVER HAVE THE ANIMALS

Never have the animals been in greater need of human compassion.

HAVE I LEFT THE EAGLE TO SOAR IN FREEDOM?

The time will soon be here when my grandchild will long for the cry of a loon, the flash of a salmon, the whisper of spruce needles, or the screech of an eagle. But he will not make friends with any of these creatures and when his heart aches with longing he will curse me.

Have I done all to keep the air fresh? Have I cared enough about the water? Have I left the eagle to soar in freedom?

Have I done everything I could to earn my grandchild's fondness?

THERE IS A LONGING

There is a longing among all people and creatures to have a sense of purpose and worth. To satisfy that common longing in all of us we must respect each other.

In the olden times man and creature walked as friends who carried the beauty of the land in their hearts. Now each one of us is needed to make sure the salmon can find a place to spawn and the bear cub a tree to climb.

There is little time left and much effort needed!

PRAYER FOR MY BROTHER THE BEAR

O Great Spirit who listens to all,
I speak for my brother the bear:

Make the moon shine softly during the nights of
his childhood so that the warmth of his mother
will always be in his memory.

Make the berries grow in abundance and sweetness
so that the vigor of life will strengthen his heart and
the years of old age shall never be a burden to his body.

Let the wildflowers refresh his temperament so
that his manner will always be carefree.

Give his legs swiftness and strength so they
will always carry him to freedom.

Sharpen the senses of his ears and nose so they
will always keep harm from him.

Let only those men share his path who in their
hearts know his beauty and respect his strength so that
he will always be at home in the wilderness.

Make men praise life so that no one needs to feel
the shame that lives in a heart that has wronged.

Then my wild brother, the bear, will always have a
wilderness, as long as the sun travels the sky.

O Great Spirit, this I ask of you for my brother the bear.

THE BEAR IS CLOSEST TO MAN

When I was born my grandfather took me from
my mother and wrapped me into a black bear's
soft fur blanket.

It gave me warmth! It gave me security and comfort!
How can I be anything but grateful to the bear?
Of all the creatures he is closest to man. Yet it seems
there is little place for him now.

THE EMPTY LOON'S NEST

I have seen the sun burn off the early morning mist as many times as there are leaves on a dogwood tree. Just as often the stars have stood vigil over my dreams, and the seasons, with their coming and going, brought enough work to keep me from lamenting their passing. Many strange things have happened during my lifetime. Often I could not understand the changes. I have been angered by some, shamed by others, and saddened by many. But nothing can give me a greater feeling of loss than the way nature disappears to make room for people's pleasure.

Beyond the reeds of the lake where my cabin stands is a loon pair's nest. Season after season I have greeted their new chicks since I was a boy. I no longer go there because the sun shines on an empty nest that the rain and wind turned into a pile of sticks. The evenings are without the laughter of loons and I wonder where they are raising their young now.

Have they built their nest away from motorboats, foul-smelling water, and people who make them dive just for fun?

Is there a quiet lake
left anywhere?

Who will bring us
the messages from
the spirit world when
the loons are gone?

MY FACE IS THE LAND

Many seasons ago my arms were strong, my spine straight, my legs had swiftness, and my eyes were as good as a hawk's. People would look at my face, and all they saw in it was the face of a nameless Indian. Few people called me brother. It was my face that kept them from wanting to know me better, because it was the face of an Indian.

Yet, already then, my face was well known.

It was known to the squirrel that heard a twig break under my foot while I walked into the woods.

It was known to the porcupine that sat in the tree top and watched me pass underneath.

It was known to the raven who cawed to other creatures to tell them of my coming.

It was known to the fox who stole from my food cache and to the beaver who watched me set traps.

It was known to the bear whose den and my house were in the same forest.

It was known to the heron who taught me patience in the quest for food.

It was known to the warbler whose song filled my heart with joy.

It was known to the wind that brought me messages from other creatures and plants.

It was known to the rain that feeds the spring where
I quenched my thirst day after day.

It was known to the lakes whose waters blended with
the sky who speaks to all of freedom.

The trees also knew my face. I was told by my father
that some day, when the skin of my face takes on the
furrows of pine bark, my spirit will leave my body and
seek a new home in a tree.

But like the wolf that soon will be gone from here,
my face is the face of a vanishing kind.

You see, what is in the wilderness is in my face,
and what is in my face is in the wilderness.

My Face is the Land!

If you misunderstand one you will neglect the other!

If you harm one you scar the other!

If you despise one you will disgrace the other!

If you shame one you will cause the other to weep!

If you look at one and cannot call its name you will never
know the other!

But how can you not know my face?

How can you not know the land?

Is it not all around you?

Is it not part of all you do and live for?

Is it not within your heart, where the yearning for
brotherhood takes its beginning?

Are we not all living in times of enlightenment
when no one should have a nameless face any longer,
not even an Indian?

Now that my hair has the color of moonlight and
my voice sounds like gentle winds blowing on dry leaves
my face is known everywhere because of the magic of films.
People point at me and say with admiration: Chief Dan
George. But how many of my brothers still have nameless
faces because they are Indians, as I once did before you
knew me as Chief Dan George?

I'VE TRIED TO BE AN INDIAN

Let no one deny me the right to say that
I've tried to be an Indian.

In the White Man's world I found it difficult,
but I've tried.

I've tried to care for my people and showed my
concern as Chief Dan George, not how others
wished me to show it.

Can the deer climb the tree like a raccoon?
There will always be someone who confuses the
deer with the raccoon, but such a person has
slow eyes and a quick tongue.

And if someone says I have not been Indian enough
he will never know how much I've tried.

A CHILD'S TRUST

A child's trust in a grown-up shows in the touch of his hand.

LET NATURE BE

Is it really important for a boy to learn the name of a wild animal, what it eats, where it lives, and how it rears its young while at the same time the boy never gets to live near the animal? Would it not be better to let nature be, and let the boy live with unspoiled affection for all creatures, instead of teaching him to boast of knowledge?

THE ONLY THING

The only thing the
world really needs is for
every child to grow up
in happiness.

TO A NATIVE TEENAGER

You are unhappy because
you live far from the city
that promises everything and
you think yourself to be poor
because you live among your people.

But when you live like
a person of city breeding
you will not hear the plants say:
eat off me,
nor will you take
from the animals because of hunger.

The ground will be so hard
that you will want to run
from place to place, and
when you have gone too far
there will be no moss to rest on,
nor will your back find
a tree to lean against.

Your thirsty throat
will long to savor water
from the cup of your hand;
instead the liquid that lives in a bottle
will burn your tongue,
soften your mind,
and make your heart ache
for the sweetness of spring water.

Tears will keep your eyes moist
because a thousand small suns
that never come nor go
flicker everywhere.
The wind will not carry
messages from land to land,
and the odor of countless machines
will press on your chest
like the smell of a thousand angry skunks.

You will look at the sky
to pray for soft rain;
instead you will find
above the tree tops
lives another city
that stands between you
and the guidance of stars,

and you will wonder where city people
keep their dead.

A longing will rise in your heart
for the days of your boyhood, and
your fingers will grip the sacred tooth
you hid in your coat pocket.
But the train that carried you into
the city never brought the spirit along
that guides lost hunters through the woods.

Again and again your eyes will try to see
the evening dripping off the sun
like wild honey and your nostrils
will quiver for the scent of water
that tumbled through the canyons
of your childhood.

You'll stand at a corner
amidst the noise
and bow your head in despair
because you are humbled
by the desire to touch
your father's canoe
that he carved when you were born.

Wherever you look
there is nothing your eyes know,
and when weakness settles into your legs
you will recognize your brother
by the shadow his hunched body casts
in the corner of a street,
in a city where people walk
without seeing the tears
in each other's eyes.

WHEN DEATH COMES

Death will be gentle with me. Like an old friend dropping in to see me and asking me to come along for a stroll towards the sun. I will not hesitate to entrust myself into his company. I will not pause in my steps to look back.

Or perhaps it will come while I am sitting in my soft chair, wrapped in my blanket. I will not sigh, so that the others can go on with their business thinking me to be asleep.

I will know then what I always suspected, that death is not a mystery but a guide to birth. Birth—everything begins with it: child, plant, river, earth and sun, stars and beyond ... and then there is that which we do not see or hear, the spirit life that some do fear.

THE EARTH WAITS FOR ME

Nights bring me hindsight,
days bring me doing,
tomorrows bring me wishes,
yesterdays bring me wisdom,
the moon vanity,
the sky longing,
the sun fear,
and the earth?
It waits for me.

A MAN

A man who cannot be
moved by a child's sorrow
will only be remembered
with scorn.

THE WOLF

The wolf has been driven from the land.
Without him the wolf clan cannot celebrate
the wolf ceremony. To lose a ceremony is
to lose the past.

THE WOLF CEREMONY

I wanted to give something of my past to my grandson. So I took him into the woods, to a quiet spot. Seated at my feet he listened as I told him of the powers that were given to each creature. He moved not a muscle as I explained how the woods had always provided us with food, homes, comfort, and religion. He was awed when I related to him how the wolf became our guardian, and when I told him that I would sing the sacred wolf song over him, he was overjoyed.

In my song I appealed to the wolf to come and preside over us while I would perform the wolf ceremony so that the bondage between my grandson and the wolf would be lifelong.

I sang. In my voice was the hope that clings to
every heartbeat.

I sang. In my words were the powers I inherited from
my forefathers.

I sang. In my cupped hands lay a spruce seed—
the link to creation.

I sang. In my eyes sparkled love.

I sang. And the song floated on the sun's rays from
tree to tree.

When I had ended, it was as if the whole world listened
with us to hear the wolf's reply. We waited a long time
but none came.

Again I sang, humbly but as invitingly as I could, until my
throat ached and my voice gave out.

All of a sudden I realized why no wolves had heard my
sacred song. There were none left!

My heart filled with tears. I could no longer give my
grandson faith in the past, our past. At last I could
whisper to him: "It is finished!"

"Can I go home now?" he asked, checking his watch
to see if he would still be in time to catch his favorite
program on TV.

I watched him disappear and wept in silence.

All *is* finished!

LIFE

We are as much
alive as we keep
the earth alive.

Life and death—
a song without an ending.

LOVE 1

Only love can stop a child from hurting.

THE GREAT SPIRIT
We hurt the Great Spirit more than he hurts us!

IF YOUR SOUL SHOULD CHOOSE A TREE

The spirit world is connected to the world of breathing creatures. An old man can't be too happy about his afterlife. If his soul should choose a tree after it has left the body, what will become of it?

What future does a tree have nowadays?

I NEVER SCORNED GOD

My life has not been easy. There were many ups and downs, good times and times I lived with anger. All my anger was with people about things that mattered only to people. I never scorned God. My grandfather took great care to teach me proper respect for God.

Our children must go to school to be civilized. There they learn about churches. It seems they have been built with the purpose of finding fault with one another. When people quarrel about churches they drag God into their squabbles. My grandfather's church was not built by men; therefore he could never have taught me to quarrel with God. Our church was nature.

THE SUN

The sun makes young people move fast and slows us old people down.

A BIT OF SUNSHINE

I enjoy sitting in the sun, although it no longer warms me as much as it used to do when I was younger.

I don't look about very much, and I don't strain my ears to hear too much. There is so much that I neither like to hear nor like to see. So I just sit in the sunshine and enjoy another quiet day.

Every time I lie down to sleep I do so without knowing if another morning will come. If it comes I say: "Good morning, world!" and then I try to find a bit of sunshine.

I WISH

I wish every child can find its true path and every man knows the right way.

WISDOM

There is wisdom in youth and
there is wisdom in age.
One is loud and seeking,
the other is silent and true.

THE GRACE OF GOD

The grace of God lives in a child's happy eyes.

A CHILD

A child does not question the wrongs of grown-ups, he suffers them!

LET SOMEONE ELSE

I've made peace with the world
and am grateful for everything.
Let someone else greet the next spring
with pleasure;
let someone else wrestle with another summer;
let someone else marvel over autumn's gifts;
let someone else say: "Life is good!"

TO A CHILD

May the stars carry your sadness away,
may the flowers fill your heart with beauty,
may hope forever wipe away your tears,
and, above all, may silence make you strong.

I WOULD BE A SAD MAN

I would be a sad man
if it were not for the hope
I see in my grandchild's eyes.

MEN

Men who do not keep the earth sacred
create much sorrow.

Grandchild, keep the eagle and the memory
of me in your heart, so that both can remain aloft
in peace, and together they will cry not of pain
but of joy!

LOVE II

It is hard for a child
not to be afraid,

It is impossible for a child
not to be confused.

Our love can make a child
look ahead with confidence.

THE DRUM HAS FALLEN SILENT

The drum has fallen silent,
the rattle lies broken,
the song has been forgotten—
my hands so feeble,
my voice so faint,
my eyes so full of tears—
O my grandson,
what will you remember me by?

ONCE MORE

Once more
    I like to hear water murmur of earth—

Once more
    I like to touch a child to feel beyond today—

Once more
    I like to taste a tree's sap to remember
    the strength of spring—

Once more
    I like to see the color of happiness
    to know the deathman's song will please me.

Then, O Earth,
    I shall be ready to return to you what little
    I have left from all the years of taking from you.

EPILOGUE
by Helmut Hirnschall

THE VICISSITUDES OF LIFE dealt Chief Dan George many a blow; the first was that he was born Indian. Like many other Indigenous people, he lived in poverty most of his life. His Indian looks were his liability. When he reached his early sixties, this liability became his fortune; the Hollywood dream-makers discovered his face and turned it into a profitable asset. His quiet assertion, his whispering voice, his cascading white hair, his furrowed face with the gentle smile became a trademark for celluloid success.

Unlike many other people who are lured to fame and fortune by television or movies, Chief Dan George remained unspoiled. He retained his simple lifestyle and his faith in the principles that had guided him before. He continued to show respect for the Indigenous ways and nature, and above all he maintained his abiding love for his wife and family.

When the Chief received an Academy Award nomination for his performance in *Little Big Man*, he and his wife planned to attend the ceremonies in Los Angeles together. Unfortunately, she became seriously ill. She insisted that he go to Los Angeles without her and watched the ceremonies on her television from her sickbed. Her pride in him momentarily eased her pain. Death took her from him at a time when he ached to share his happiness with her.

In the following years, the Chief's star rose higher, and he acted before the camera next to such screen giants as Bob Hope, Glenn Ford, David Carradine, Clint Eastwood, Dennis Weaver, Art Carney, and Suzanne Sommers, to name just a few. He could not fully enjoy his success, however, because his wife was no longer a part of it. Without her, he was no longer whole. His devotion to his wife, his longing to be with her, became stronger with every passing year. Near the end of his life he had withdrawn into the great emptiness her absence had created.

The last time I visited Chief Dan George I found him sitting in a chair in front of his house. A blanket kept him snug, the sun caressed him with warmth, the air bore the fragrance of summer. His eyes were closed, and so I approached him quietly. I dared not call his name or touch him lest I disturb his dreams. I wondered which lines in his face had been carved by hardships and which lines had been left behind by happiness. The skin followed closely the contours of his cheekbones, the mouth—emptied of its teeth—seemed without lips. The last few months had weaned so much from his body, everything about him said: It is time for me to let go. I remembered a dream I had had over a year ago. In it I saw him walk up the garden path to my house. At the front door we carried on a telepathic conversation. Shaking my hand, he declined to come inside and "told" me that he had some to say goodbye. I had been a good friend, and he thanked me for sharing his path. He would die in September.

During my waking hours I silenced my dream with doubts about its message. September came and went, and life stayed with him. I was glad my dream was no prophecy, and, like all other dreams before, this one too was quickly forgotten.

As I looked at him sitting in the chair while the sunlight played on his thin, white hair, a deep sadness took hold of me. Suddenly I knew my dream would be true; another September, only weeks away, would never end for him.

His eyes remained closed, but he seemed aware of me. Perhaps he had known all along that I was standing there watching him. He beckoned me to sit next to him, and I knew he wanted me to live out the words that he had dictated to me months earlier:

Touch my hand
before my voice will falter,
sit with me
until the shadows go,
then smile ...

Chief Dan George died the way he had always lived: quietly. His soul slipped from his sleeping body during the night of September 23, 1981.

As a small child he had watched his grandfather relocate their ancestors' bones and family relics. The new gravesite was farther up the Burrard Inlet, and the bones were transported in a canoe. As his grandfather paddled up the inlet, seven porpoises appeared and followed alongside the canoe. Just before the canoe arrived at the shore where the new burial grounds were, the porpoises swam several times around the canoe and then dove and were never seen again. Dan George was told that the souls of his forefathers had been in those porpoises.

When Chief Dan George was buried, family and friends watched in awe as an eagle appeared overhead and flew, in silent circles. After the grave had swallowed the casket, the eagle disappeared into the clouds.

*Lots of Love and Respect
May the Great Spirit
Love and Protect you
to the End of time
Hatha Squalem, te na thau*

*Chief Dan George
Tanyal, Stalaston*

RELATED TITLES

View all Hancock House titles at hancockhouse.com

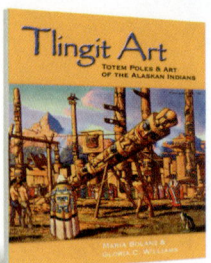

Tlingit Art
Maria Bolanz
Gloria C Williams
ISBN 9780888395092 SC
ISBN 9780888395283 HC

Indigenous Herbs
Raymond Stark
ISBN 9780888390776 SC

Potlatch People
Mildred Valley Thornton
ISBN 9780888394910 SC

The Missing Caribou Hide
Wendy Stephenson
Cecilia Judas
ISBN 9780888397621 SC

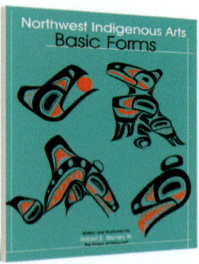

Northwest Indigenous Arts: Basic Forms
Robert Stanley, Sr.
ISBN 9780888395061 SC

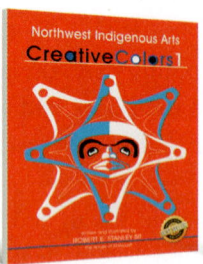

Northwest Indigenous Arts: Creative Colors I
Robert Stanley, Sr
ISBN 9780888395320 SC

Northwest Indigenous Arts: Creative Colors II
Robert Stanley, Sr
ISBN 9780888395337 SC

Burnt Snow
Kieran Moore
ISBN 9780888393562 HC
ISBN 9780888393098 SC

Now You Know Me
Joe Gallagher
John Matterson
ISBN 9780888397829 SC

Community Healing
Geneva Ensign
ISBN 9780888390578 SC

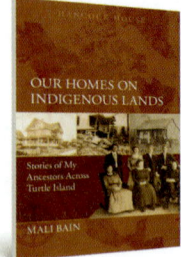

Our Homes on Indigenous Lands
Mali Bain
ISBN 9780888397416 SC

Indigenous Quillworking
Christy Ann Hensler
ISBN 9780888392145 SC